Love Will Find You Elsewhere

A. N. Moore

With Illustrations by Justine Neves

Love Will Find You Elsewhere

Instagram @anmooreword

Facebook / A. N. Moore Word

Twitter @anmooreword

Cover and Chapter Illustrations with Captions: Justine Neves
Instagram- @justine_artworks
www.justineneves.com

Revisions and Editing
Amanda Shepard

ISBN: 978-1983510281

ISBN-10: 1983510289

Dedicated to the lovers, the dreamers

and the hopeless romantics.

But most importantly

to my best friend, my wife, the love of my life.

Without you, this book would have never come

to fruition.

Dear Reader,

I am so proud to present *Love Will Find You Elsewhere*; a poetry
book of duel personalities.

On the right side of the book is a story
written through verse. Read the right side the first time through.

The left side is a mix of poetry, written to help illustrate and enhance the narrator's journey.
The duel nature of this book will allow you, the reader, to have a different experience each
time you flip through its pages.

It should be noted that in this book there will be material
addressing the following topics:

Homosexuality

Homophobia

Coming Out

Feminism

Emotional Abuse

Sex

Self-harm

Self-Love

Mental Health

and last, but not least:

Love

Love and Light,

A. N. Moore

love will find you

They will ask
what is so special about my story

And I will look at them and say
I am not saying anything
you do not already know

I am just saying it in a way
that you want to hear

I am listening
I am here

And I do not even need to know you
in order to understand what you have been through

Love, pain, joy, disappointment, and fears
it is all here
it is in all of us
and that is the beauty
of the human condition

That, my friend, is the
human connection

Consumed to what depth, we'll see...

nowhere

Today I write of all the things
I should have said about
so many yesterdays I have
never forgotten

-inspiration

I have always been a firm believer in love
how it doesn't make sense
yet it makes everything make sense

But I am talking about the love that
makes your heart recalibrate
to the rhythm of a soulmate

I wasn't sure where to find it
or if it even exists

But I knew it was more
than what I was given
and I knew better than to trust it
based off of one kiss

In my childhood home
we never talked about love
where it comes from
what it looks like
what it means
what it does

And I have always thought that love
deserved better than that

-hopeless romantic

Romantics are just hopelessly
broken dreamers

It was never a staple
it was never something taught

We were just supposed to know that we had it
and that it was always enough

When I find love
I always thought to myself

I am going to see it
I am going to show it

I am going to shower myself in it

There was something all too familiar
about the way that you could make me laugh
two people always crossing paths
with a love not meant to last

-star-crossed

Like most other girls
I was taught early
That love looks like
the princess and prince
in those fairytale books

That love was inevitable
if you dreamt for it long enough

One day *he* would show up
my knight and shining armor

Saving me from all the bad
giving me everything that's good

What a load of shit that was

Hidden in plain sight
are those that we convinced
ourselves were angels
but who are really just
monsters in disguise

The problem is
when you read those fairytales

It's also so easy to recognize
the right one versus the wrong one

Surprise, surprise reality hits

And my God, can I tell you
nobody can tell the difference

We grow up
and here we are still waiting
for *him* to show up

Maybe *he* is this one
no, maybe *he* is that one
or maybe it isn't *him* at all

And that is the problem

But maybe
just maybe
a part of us might believe that
this thing called love
doesn't really exist at all

Tormented, thinking love
would never find me
I turned inwards
I looked for it in places it would never be
and in people not meant for me

The funny thing
about those fairytales
they do not tell you
how to love someone else

The funny thing about
those fairytales
they teach you that
loving someone else
may in fact trump loving yourself

So here you are
stuck with all this magical love
but you have no idea where to start

Instead of with yourself
you start trying to love someone else

She was a wild love;
to love her was to let her be free

They also do not tell you
that nobody really looks
like that or acts like that

Those princesses
and that one of a kind prince
really do not exist

But the problem is
even when we are grown up
we still expect *them* to show up

We want everything to
be like those dreams
that fantasy

We force those fairytales to shape our reality

There is something about expectations
that only breeds resentment

Love Will Find You Elsewhere

Dear brown-eyed girl
never lose sight of the love
deep inside your soul

-the world needs more lovers like you

A. N. Moore

Those damn books

Never showed the type of love
I needed to see

So as a young girl
when I began to realize
I loved differently

It really took a toll on me

-no role models

Do not get discouraged, darling
your soul was not made to satisfy them

-the promise

So when I found myself
pining over a woman

The way that others did a man

I rejected myself
instead of accepting myself

Instead of coming out

I hid

There is no greater anguish
than knowing you have the potential
to swim but you choose to sink
just to please everyone else
instead of yourself

When the first girl
I knew to ever come out
left school crying

I knew that hiding
was what I should
continue to do

Girls like boys
Boys like girls

Everyone repeats it like a mantra

Girls like boys
Boys like girls

I start saying it too
trying to convince my heart
that this is *my* truth

-mantra

Courage does not only belong to lions
it belongs to those who are a part of the ocean
and decided to make their own current
when it told them to be still and silent

For years I sat there
thinking about the girl
that never returned to school

While I still sat in the closet
she was out and proud

I tried having boyfriends
but that word never sat right
on my tongue

I could never kiss one
no matter how pressured I was

Repeating that mantra in my head
it still had not stuck

Clinging to everyone's expectations
of who or what you should be
is the same thing as fruit
that does not fall from the tree

-unfulfilled destiny

The word boyfriend
is hard to swallow
it's even harder to chew
a word that should come naturally
feels like an unfamiliar food

-no thank you

I kept picking up the pieces of my past
like the dandelions of my youth
each time blowing a wish
for things to change
for things to be different;
sometimes we forget that dandelions
are in full bloom too
and wishes will not change the
destiny within your truth

A. N. Moore

The first girl
that gave me butterflies
was the first girl
that told me I was just like her

I asked her what she meant
and she made a rainbow with her hands

I went home that night
half-way delighted
the other half panicked

Is it seeping through my skin

Did someone write the word on my forehead

How did she know what my heart had known all along

That night I wished for my tears to flood these feelings out of me

That is the thing nobody really wants to admit
the best kind of love is
unexplainable
incomparable
almost feels unobtainable

It is the kind of love where words
just don't seem to fit

-searching

A. N. Moore

I begged her to tell me
how she knew what she knew

She said it was something she had

Kind of like a sixth sense
I would one day get it, too

-gay-dar

They told me to bare my soul
in black and white
I told them I wanted to bare
my soul in colors;
my love won

-*pride*

That day, I went home
to my journal

I scribbled out the mantra
and rewrote this instead:

Some girls like boys
Some boys like girls

And I am not one of them

-girls like girls, too

Let me save myself
you do not need to save me
it is not your job
nor your destiny

If I don't do it myself
with my own two hands
I will only become a reflection
of who you thought I should be
instead of who I truly am

-no knights, no shining armor

A. N. Moore

One day I went to the library
and I found a friend who understood
what I was going through

It was a short chapter book
about a girl who loved a girl

And I finally found a book
that put those fairytales to shame

-a real role model

Comfort zones are just the devil's playground
they convince you that you can live with *this*
and that you don't deserve *that*

The feeling in the pit of your stomach;
let it be your catalyst for change

-you deserve better

Despite my newfound revelations
and coming into my own
I felt sick to my stomach

The kind where you know something
bad is going to happen
but you also know
there is no way to stop it

You broke the promise
the unwritten rule
so I have to learn
the hard way
that not everything
works out as much as I might want it to

-(un)conditional love

A. N. Moore

Some people are lucky
they can go to everyone and open up
and talk about anything and everything

That never felt like a door I could open
it was not a line
that I felt comfortable
enough to cross

So when it came time for me to
come out from hiding

I not only had the slightest idea
of how to approach it

I had no idea what I was going
to do if they did not approve of it

And a huge part of me knew that they wouldn't

I wish we could have an open conversation
but you only want to share your opinions
when I just need someone to listen

-do you hear me?

Everyone says love is unconditional
and maybe it is
for some people

But you will never understand
what it's like telling everyone

You like women instead of men
it's like tossing a quarter

Calling heads or tales
a fifty-fifty chance
that this love
may or may not be based on condition

Keep fighting for your truth
you will become stronger because of it

-love will always win in the end

I've never had a tear soaked pillow
quite as soaked as it was that night
I spoke my truth

When I was told
that it was only right
to keep living a lie

It will be better for everyone
they said

But what about me
nobody cared if I was alright

-back in the closet

Love Will Find You Elsewhere

It is easy using words as hateful venom
instead of a loving antidote;
speak from hate and you are in control
speak from love and your vulnerabilities show

-fine lines

A. N. Moore

For the next
couple of days

I wondered how it would feel

To empty myself
of all the pain
regret
disappointment

I wondered how it would feel
to bleed away
the sorrow
the heartache
the worry

A clean slate
to prove to
everyone that
I am worthy

-self-harm

We can wish for it to go away
the heartache
the pains
the emotions that seem to
devour us whole
for days on end
emotions like these demand to stay
to make the good a little sweeter
the love a little stronger;
silver linings everywhere

-perspective

I go to the doctor and exclaim
my head
my head
it is a mess
it just does not feel right

I knew the answer of course
go to someone and work it out

It is okay
depression happens
sadness can and will fade

Except that answer never came

She gave me a pill
side-effects included
this should do the trick

Yes
sure
why not
put a Band-Aid over it
instead of getting to the root of it

-too many quick fixes

So I stood before people
seeking validation
time and time again
without questioning
why I felt the need to
rise and fall on their standards
instead of my own

-self-worth

When you start hating yourself
it becomes really easy
to point out everything
that is wrong with you

It becomes a habit
an addiction

Trying to get yourself
out of this self-loathing
proves to be one long road to recovery

-and I am still learning

What were you running from
when you told me you loved me
and left anyway
What were you afraid of
when I told you to stay?

-3:00 am thoughts

A. N. Moore

A part of me knew
that the relationships I had

With everyone I thought I knew
were going to change
were going to fade

And my biggest mistake
was going to be holding onto them
instead of setting them free

I can no longer live my life
to meet your expectations
when I have a life to live
that is very much my own
let me speak my truth
when I say that love is love

-are you listening now?

A. N. Moore

Why does my sexuality
make everyone uncomfortable

The cliché questions and comments
are written all over their faces

But you are too pretty

you cannot really be gay

What happened to you

that forced you to be this way

It is so unnatural for you

what a waste

You don't look like a lesbian

what gender role do you play

I never asked for your approval in the first place

*-I've lost count as to how many times I've had this
conversation*

Holding onto something tighter
does not guarantee that it won't go away

Let it thrive
let it grow
all on its own

If it doesn't stay
it is better that it walked away

That is one thing
I wish I had learned sooner

People will not change
when you beg them too

People will not understand
when you force them too

Change only comes to someone
when they feel in their heart
it is the right thing to do

Never hurt yourself
never punish yourself
for not being able to do something
that a person is going to have to decide
to do on their own

-change

What a shame it is to lose something
to know what you had
when you had that something

What a shame it is to lose out on loving you

-loss

A. N. Moore

I still cry for every girl
who fell in love with another
long before they knew it
was okay to feel this way

All this young love
never given the chance to breathe
because of society's inability
to get over its insecurities
about love being more than what
we have been lead to believe

I am one of you, too

-community

Pick me, then pick me apart (love me not)

somewhere

I never wanted to sacrifice
understanding myself
just so that others could
understand me

-self-appreciation

A. N. Moore

I am growing
and it is scary

I am out of my comfort zone
it's crawling out of my skin

I am learning to love myself
for exactly who I am

I am on the verge of a breakthrough
no longer living my life to please you

-growing pains

Beauty was found
in her unapologetic truth;
she wasn't trying to be
anything but herself
and that alone
made her magical

There is something so beautiful
about a heart pounding the first time
it finds itself mesmerized

The way her wine stained lips
curled over her one of a kind smile

She was killing me
yet saving me
all at the same damn time

-crush

I wish we would just take these moments
and understand that everyone
is fishing but not everyone
is meant to reel you into shore

Remember, there are just as many
fisherman as there are fish in the sea

-don't take the bait

I will be the first to admit
when I first fell in love

I fell way too fast
because her lips
were the first lips
I wanted to kiss back

Her hands felt like home
in the comfort of my own

Remember when we were nothing more
than a couple of kids
Chasing this feeling
we knew was so fleeting

-young love

For a long time
it was just me and her

This new love
this new experience

It was all so freeing
but I wanted that freedom
to be spread all over me

So I started sharing this love

What a relief it was

Love Will Find You Elsewhere

Is that how you still
maintain your
dignity;

Turning us into your unobtainable fantasy

I can turn you into a stereotype too:

You
a screen
your hand between your knees
while you sit there and wonder

-why you can't have me

The first thing I learned
when I started embracing my
sexuality was that when people looked at me
one too many thoughts turned dirty

As if my private bed room
was exposed for the world to see

lesbian

Sugar coated in filthy-fantasies
rolling off the tongue of men
like a challenge they could win

Do you really think
that highly of yourself
and that less of me
to assume your manhood is what is
going to make or break my identity;
I hope your arrogance and ignorance
make for great company

A. N. Moore

One too many times
I did not fit *the stereotype*

One too many times
I was told that I just needed
to be shown what it feels
like to be with a *real* man

Like my long hair and dresses
made me any less of a lesbian

-*femme*

I am not a challenge
nor am I a prize to be won
I am not your ego boost
do not expect to dip
yourself in my honey
to make a mockery out of me
just because you are uncomfortable
that this body does not lust for you

A. N. Moore

Do you want to know
the funny thing about men

They did not want me
until they knew
that I did not want them

So they showed me their manhood
tucked away in tiny screens

Hoping to find answers
as to why it was her
and not them
who made my fingers
dance between my knees

-emasculation

Hope blooms like wild flowers
in the hearts of the hopeless romantics;
loving you will either water my roots
or pick me apart for the pretty little thing
that I am and leave me wilting

-50/50 chance

For the record I said
I love you
and I meant it

At least I thought I did
but as soon as I did

I got the feeling
that something was
going to go bad again

-intuition

It is when you are falling in love
to fall out of your insecurities
that you are in treacherous territory

She said there is a difference
you know

Between "I love you" and "love you"

There is something so
vulnerable about including the "I"

The emotion is connected to you
and you are very much attached to that love

That night all I wanted to do
was spill out all the "I love yous"
with an emphasis on the "I"
the me
the we

This identity of us
became the reason I breathed
I was addicted to this feeling
without really thinking
that I could have been

-speaking too soon

A star must explode before it is born
the same way you must learn
to walk before you can run
your heart will want to call it love
before you have really found the one

-trust the process

A. N. Moore

Young love
will always be a dangerous love

You get so caught up
in the idea of love
that you start making excuses
for this love being the right love

Because you don't know of a different love

How it works
what is right
what is wrong

Sometimes it will take years
for you to understand
that this love
never deserved the title
in the first place

The scary thing is
I could not tell you
if it was the real thing or
if I was just drunk off
the idea of loving someone
What a sad truth
to be so lonely
that even a wrong love
is better than no love at all

-filling the void

Because when you are young
you are so desperate to call it love
way too soon

When the heart is flooded with
the kissing
the stolen glances

And the late night obsessing

But how quickly it all fades
when you think the magic
has gone away

Who are we trying to kid
it is not love you are after
you are just chasing lust

And it is so easy to forget
that there is a difference

-word choice

Remember, nobody has ever ripped
apart a garden of roses
and left with clean hands
roses have thorns
and they do not play nice with hands
not meant to hold them

-be a rose

A. N. Moore

The first time
the words
I love you

Are used to make
demands of you

Run.

I tried leaving my own demons
just so I could dance with yours
misery loves company

A. N. Moore

I didn't run
like I should've

The first time I understood
how selfish love could be
was when I sat beside you and you did not care
to notice that you were the only one happy

-selfish

A. N. Moore

When love is selfish
it takes your heart
and holds it hostage

Too often
it was a question
of why you were happy
and I wasn't

Too often I brushed the answer off
because after all
this was love
wasn't it?

So as you dipped your tongue in me
as your fingers grazed my skin
I was empty

I turned off the lights
I closed the shutters
the music fell silent
and you ripped apart my home

But you were happy
it didn't matter that I wasn't

How sudden did it happen
this love becoming a sacrifice?

Love Will Find You Elsewhere

You made a mistake
when you thought
that what rests
between her thighs
was more beautiful
than the thoughts that occupy her mind

-more than my body

A. N. Moore

You told me I was perfect
until I would not give it up

I love yous
became twisted into
demands of you need to

Insecure
Immature
Unwillingly

You unraveled me
before I was ready to be undone

We lied to ourselves
while lying next to each other
trying to make up ways
to say that what we shared
was the truth

-reality

But that is the thing
when you do not know any better

Hands that once tenderly held my heart

Started turning it black and blue
but I always swore it would get better

I wonder how you will tell our story
how you will navigate from beginning to end
do you captivate your audience
by making a monster out of me
I will not make a villain out of you
I know we all carry different versions of the same story;
but everyone should know that ours is a tragedy

-versions

And even after I began questioning
how this love had
turned so sour
at the hands of someone
who was once
so tender

I made the terrible mistake
of blaming myself
instead of blaming you

And maybe it is some cosmic design
to fall in love with darkness first
so when the light inevitably
comes to conquer the sorrow
your heart will be quicker to surrender
rather than put up the fight

A. N. Moore

So you say sorry
Again, I forgive you

Because the "I love yous"
you feed me
made me
feel like I am
obligated to

You are only holding yourself back
If you know you are watering
your insecurities like weeds
and still expect anything else to grow there

And that is the trouble
with those three words

We are taught to
say it to others

But never told
we need to start saying it
to ourselves first

This love turned into
a game of give and take;
me giving all of myself
you taking everything
and leaving crumbs

Because if I learned
what I should have
I would have never
let you use those words
as a weapon against me

-manipulation

How did we let this happen
our desperation for this emotion
let it be misused, abused, and tossed
around in mediocrity and cheap
knock-off versions

-love in this generation

You told me you were kissing away the pain
instead you sent poison through my veins

Slowly but surely
I became less of the person
I was meant to be

You liar
you cheat
you were nothing but a monster
I had mistaken for the real thing

-be wise with the words 'I love you'

Do not let anyone fool you
love has never been synonymous with control

-antonyms

The person you are now
is the not the same person
I thought I fell in love with

You began towering over
the woman I was supposed to be

Controlling

You fenced me in
doubting my loyalty
stifling my spirit
opportunities were traded for barriers

Power

Excuse me but did you ever even hear me

Poison

This is not the real me
stop saying you love me
when it is only on condition

What I do
What I say
What I wear
Who I am

Is not contingent on gaining your permission

-lesson

Nothing is wasted more than a voice
that has been scared silent
by people who are scared of its power

-speak up

I have words forming
in the back of my throat
wanting to escape
just so they can rescue me
from the pain

And I finally let them
I want to spill them all over the floor
let them role off my tongue
let them drip from my lips

So easy
yet so difficult
to let the first one escape from them

My voice crackles
at first, my hands shake
but then it comes billowing out of me

No.

I said it again

No.
            -and I will say it again and again and again

We got tossed in vicious cycles of "I love yous"
without ever really knowing how to love ourselves
first

-the biggest mistake

Sometimes
I find myself
still searching
for the moment
where it all
went wrong;

Me and you
so innocent

... And there is was

-innocence

And maybe the emptiness you feel now
has finally caught up to you
reminding you to watch what
pieces of yourself you choose to give away

A. N. Moore

Not long after it had started
did it end

At least that is what I thought
but weeks turned to months
and months turned to a year

I looked at myself in the mirror one day
and realized I did not recognize
my own reflection

Was it me
who really allowed you to reduce
myself to nothing;
that question alone
makes me realize
I am so far away from
my very own soul

Tell me
did you still find
my broken spirit
and my tear stained eyes attractive

Did it turn you on
knowing that I was nothing
but a shell of
who I once was

That must be how you like your women

-questions

And I should have known
that by feeding myself
with your words and your opinions
that one day I would look at myself
and only see the negatives

Do you remember
how many times
you fed my insecurities
instead of my heart

How many times
I kept you around
after you failed to be there for me

How many times I decided
to tear myself apart
trying to be exactly what
you said you wanted and needed

Tell me,
how many times...

-one too many

Maybe it was not about forgiveness
but about understanding
everything happened for a reason
and you were essential to my growth
you made me see what I could be on my own

-be gracious to those who hurt you, they help shape you

But there is beauty
in hitting rock bottom
there is more room to grow
and the first thing
I knew I needed to outgrow

-was you

There is beauty and there is charm
in remembering your worth

And there is so much power
in never settling for less than you deserve

And even though
we had to end that way
and as much as I'd like
to say you were a mistake
it does not feel right
calling you that

Because I know you
and you will find
your way out of this
and into excuses

So I will call you a lesson instead

Fall where it may, at least I've been flying

anywhere

Love Will Find You Elsewhere

Nothing felt familiar
it all felt alien, foreign even;
that is how you know you have not been
yourself for so long
when your skin is not your skin
you are a stranger from a distant land
trying to recover and recollect
on the pieces of yourself
before you found yourself in the enemy's hands

-amnesia

For a long time
after I had shed you
from my skin

I punished myself
for not knowing sooner
that I should have never
fallen for you like I did

Some loves are temporary
do not break your own heart
forcing forever to fit
one size does not fit all
when it comes to sharing your soul

A. N. Moore

For the record
love should scare the shit out of you

It messes people up

Gay
Straight
Bi
Whatever

Love is one hell of a drug to all of us

Anytime you are broken
piece by piece
part by part
give yourself permission to heal
no one can grow if their heart
is constantly in a war zone

What you learn
over time
is that you can love
just about anyone

And no matter who you are with
you will call them
the one

Because that is what you do
it is your own little reassurance
that who you are with
is the only one
you should be with

But with you
I was so sure
that this was true

You were my only *one* for so long

And I didn't want to
go through a dozen other *ones*

Because somehow I knew
I would still only be searching for you

The sun could not answer her
when she asked about her pain
it was the moon who cradled her
broken spirit and gave her wings
it was then she understood
darkness can bring to light
beauty that is more than skin deep

So I have decided
that the only one
I'm going to love
right now

Is myself

Because I deserve it

I wish I would have learned how to self-sooth
it would have saved me
from reaching out to someone who
was not truly meant for me

I suffered just to get the comfort
I should have been able to give myself

-reflection

A. N. Moore

I see a therapist
which is the right
thing to do

And all of my friends
act like it is so taboo

Which is something I will never understand
I am trying to rebuild this home

There is nothing wrong with
needing a little help to dig down
deep into my roots

Tear out all the rotten decay
and cultivate the love
deeply rooted inside these bones

-mental health

No longer can negativity live here
there is too much love
blooming deep inside my soul

She sat there and made me reflect on the
scared little girl that still stays buried inside

I wept
until I remembered the woman
I am supposed to become

I am stronger
than the person who broke me
I cannot control what happened to me
only how I let this pain define me

-therapy 101

Love Will Find You Elsewhere

While searching for myself
I kept finding traces of you

-shedding my skin

A. N. Moore

When I left you
I wasn't expecting
to see your ghost
every time I looked in the mirror

The therapist asks me
to tell her what I see

But I have gotten so
out of practice of being
who I should be
after practicing so long
to be what you expected of me

That is what the wrong ones do
convince you they are the right one
while they pick you apart until you are nothing
but pretty little petals, scattered across the floor;
a mere half of what you once were

A. N. Moore

One day
the therapist asks me
to go buy myself flowers

I buy a dozen sunflowers
they are happy and friendly
I pick them apart

And lay them on
every inch of me
that still cries for you

And I beg myself
to love myself

I will not drown in the sorrows of today
I have too much strength to carry on
to my many tomorrows
I will not sink
I will rise
and I will bloom

I cried
for what seemed
like days on end

The flower petals wilted
and when there were
no more tears to be shed

I told myself that this is the end of it

Tears for you
were not going
to help me bloom

I won't give you my heart
you will earn my heart
but only if you are worthy of all that I am

-standards

The little voice inside my head
gradually began saying
yes, I can

Instead of no, I can't
The minute I realized
that learning how to love
all began with loving
all the parts of me
that only I would understand

The parts you carelessly
marked as unworthy
of the little love you could give

I guess I will say that it's funny
the way it all fell apart

I will shout-out the clichés
just to comfort the awkward nature
of you and me

And how we claimed to be able to stand the rain
but really couldn't even find
the sunshine in our partly cloudy skies

That familiar song
played again today

It reverberated the heart strings
that I had for sometime
considered broken

It was that same old song
the one you always used to sing

The one I used to love
and used to play as I day dreamed
about your smile and us holding hands

How different it all is now
the way it makes me cringe

The way it makes me stop dead in my tracks
instead of the way it used to make me dance

Music
such a beautiful tragedy
the way it carries all those
broken memories
in its melody

A person will tell you
all you need to know
without saying a single word
sometimes silence is the loudest
noise our heart knows

I used to enjoy
all those songs
you used to send to me

To tell me how much
you loved me
in verses
you could not articulate
on your own

But lately I have had
no greater friend than silence

The truth is
you deserve better
than what most people
are willing to give

A balancing act
that is all it was
love and hate
hate and love

A thin line I walked across
whenever my thoughts
drifted to memories of us

I can't make up my mind
the devil is in the details

After a reckless love
a fragile heart
just needs to hear
its own heartbeat
in order to recalibrate
back to its own rhythm

Everyone starts telling me
to pick up the bad habit
of drowning out my sorrows
on someone new

Which seems ridiculous
considering I just let go of you

While everyone is getting wasted
on temporary loves

I ran warm bath water
soaked my bones in honey and eucalyptus

I was not in the mood to please anybody
if I could not please myself

-renewed

There is something so everlasting
about temporary people

-memories that haunt me

A. N. Moore

I haven't navigated my own body
in so long that no part of it
feels like it is worthy of my hands

Your haunting touch
hovers over me in jealousy

You need to know that you are enough;
that being enough for yourself
is more important than being enough for someone else

-stop feeling guilty for this

You have to learn to be alone

Be okay with just yourself
and no one else

Because people are
one hell of a distraction

Just like a glass of wine
or two, four, six, eight

However many distractions it takes
they still will not drown out the
weight of your pain

To be at peace
let yourself breathe
without the help of anyone or anything

In time you will see yourself heal

-meditation

You cannot be a stranger
to your own heartbeat
and expect someone else
to understand it's song

-friendly reminder

A. N. Moore

I had a friend tell me today
that I was in big trouble
for giving so much of
myself away

I don't even know
how to love myself

How can anyone
know what they

Want
Need
Deserve

If they haven't
watered their own garden
fed their own soul

Love Will Find You Elsewhere

Never forget that
you are made of oceans
and that you never needed anything
but your own two hands
to bring about a hurricane

Go ahead and start learning
how to please yourself

"Taste your own damn honey," she said

So the next time anyone demands
your sweetness
you can tell them
not every honeybee
deserves the Queen

-I taste freedom

I just needed someone whose love
could ignite my soul
the same way their touch
could ignite my skin

A. N. Moore

That night I learned just
how to please myself

In ways that you never could

And I didn't have to fake it

-solo I

Have a little faith in yourself
your heart isn't going
to steer you wrong
what lies ahead
is a lesson or a blessing

-reminder

A. N. Moore

The next day
I walked into the sun;
the flowers
and the trees
were in awe of me

-blooming

You are now a distant memory
you are now a passing thought
a reminder of all the time I wasted
in trying to make you
something you were not

A. N. Moore

It is weird thinking about you
but the more I do
the more I realize
how much I did not really know you

And the more I understand
how little I really knew of myself

It is no wonder that we could not outlast the
promise of an everlasting love

It was the way she looked at me and laughed
that hint of desire mixed with unmistakable happiness;
irresistible
pure bliss

A. N. Moore

I met a woman
And those butterflies
dusted off their wings
and they fluttered again

An old familiar feeling
sparked by someone new

She chose to run against the wind
she did not fret about being
unlike all the rest
all she wanted was a challenge
all she needed was a change
so she kept on running
leaving everything behind but her name

A. N. Moore

I finally threw out
the last remaining pictures
of me and you;
I danced that night
because I could finally
picture my life
and it didn't include you

-redemption

You are a lioness;
it is a victory
to remain soft
to remain gentle
after so much of you
has needed you to show your teeth

How typical it was
that I would run into you
in the process of getting over you

I'm not surprised, really
in fact, I feel empowered, really

Because it finally felt great to say
what was on my mind

-closure

The difference was in the way
I put myself together
after you tore me apart

-I am not the same girl you used to know

A. N. Moore

And you broke me
you didn't know it
or maybe you did

And the only thing you deserve
to know now
is that I am hurting
but I am healing

You want answers to things
I have since stored away to be
forgotten

These wounds have finally scabbed over; I
have never been one to pull anything back
apart once it is mended

-there, I said it, part I

I no longer waste my energy on what
you choose to see in me

For your opinion means so little to me

At the end of the day
who I am to myself
is all that matters

I am beautiful
I am strong
I am phenomenal

-I am woman

Quit your bullshit
stop trying to claw your way back
your pitiful apologies
your half-hearted attempts
to reconcile without reflecting
on what you did

You didn't need me
only your ego did

Claiming me self-righteous
as you refuse to look at your own reflection

You are not looking to change anything
and that is fine, but do not get upset
when you see I've already shed you from my skin

-there, I said it, part II

My story does not lie in the breaking
but the rebuilding of what someone
took for granted;
watch me rise
even better this time

A. N. Moore

How did I know
when the healing was through?

When I could walk into places
and see familiar faces
that were once
so precious to me and you

And realize that
even in these spaces
those memories
and that pain
were now just a part of me
not the essence of me

I was finally becoming the woman
I am supposed to be

-without you

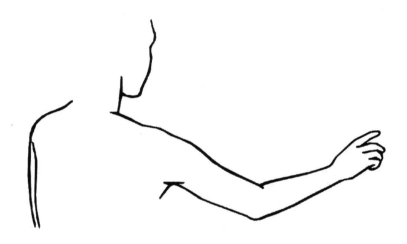

Had so much more than what my hands have carried

everywhere

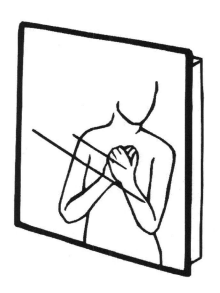

That's the thing about hands
they serve to teach you
about the world around you

What is soft
what is hard
what is good
what is bad

They work tirelessly
to reach for things that we want
and the things that we need

One of which used to be you
but they got tired of reaching for someone
who would not reach for them too

But here you are
reaching far and wide
searching for my familiar embrace

Stop reaching

Do not reach for me
these hands no longer
wish to hold you

-hands

A. N. Moore

It is amazing what a little
space and clarity can do

Time has passed
and it no longer pains me
to recall what we had been through

I am ready to move onto a love
very different than the one
I shared with you

Screw every person who decided
to only love pieces of me instead
of the masterpiece I am

-know your worth

A. N. Moore

Self-love
is soul food;
exactly what I needed
to get over you

I am all fire
the kind that
lingers in all of the
right places

The kind where anybody
who tries to flood me out
is only greeted with
a brighter flame

My embers scorch
those unworthy

I don't need a soulmate
I am everything I need
all on my own

Anybody who couldn't handle me
for the wild rage that I am
was never meant to play
with me in the first place

-confidence

No longer can I let mediocrity
stifle the magic in me
as if my magic had more
to do with you and less of me;
it is in these veins
and it is about time I remind everyone
that the world will start and end with me

-the future is female

A. N. Moore

If I can tell you anything
I have learned
it is that after a love has gone wrong

Promise yourself
to not search for it
not force it

For once
just let it find you

Why are you forcing me
to be incomplete
as if incomplete is a hot-commodity

Is it a deal breaker
is it something you need
in order to love me
or is so that you
and your ego can feel complete
just so you can tell my story for me

-stop romanticizing broken girls

But everyone does it
I don't know a person
who hasn't

We finally kick that old love
and fall too quickly
into another person's arms

Each one of them the same:
claiming to be different

-no thank you

You worry me
the way you are so jaded
that you think love is out to get you
instead of save you

Because the truth is
as much as we want to
kick the habit

Crying out "good riddance"

Our life revolves around it
we make moves
we bloom
we laugh
we cry

So much of our life
is consumed by the idea
of wanting to share
needing to love
and caring for someone

I won't believe it for a second
if someone told me
they have written it off for good

-love

I will push and push until
there is nowhere left for you to go
for this love to grow
because I am a little lost
and a lot of damage
you're fighting a hurricane;
I need someone who can
meet me eye to eye
and show me the serenity

A. N. Moore

Why do that to yourself
cut yourself off
close the curtains
and put a seal around your heart

Do not give anyone who broke your heart
or left it bruised and battered
control over you once the pain has passed
and the healing is through

Welcome the right love in
at the right time;
it will be your greatest revenge

-let love in, again

Even when we are told to grow up
we cannot help but be wild
misunderstood dreamers
carried along on the melodies of our youth
and the promise of our own happily ever after

A. N. Moore

Just like every other girl
a little part of me still
believes fate has a way
of stepping in

When you least demand it
and do not expect it

That is when love walks in

-damn those fairytales

I liked the inferno in your eyes
heavy and needy
you wanted me
and I needed you

Tempting me
and teasing me

Let me play with your fire

A. N. Moore

I saw that woman again today
the one who caught my eye
for the first time
such a long time ago

The funny thing is
each time I see her
it is like my heart
already knows her

I know nothing about her
but every fiber in my
being is telling me I need to

Swallow me whole
turn me to stardust
and a mid-summer night's dream;
your eyes so hungry for the light
after holding onto darkness for so long

A. N. Moore

I guess that gay-dar
I had received so long ago
was still operating like it should
because I saw you and I just knew;

It's a feeling
a sensation
that this girl
is just like you

-oh, trust me, I knew

She tasted like the pale moonlight
with a touch of stardust;
what an endless
summer love she was

You know, nothing is quite as nice
as the falling

The unexpected kind
where two friends
fall in love

It is the real deal
unforced, unrefined

It is raw
it is natural
it is slow
it is honey dripping off the comb

-honey

Screw timing
I hope love hits you
when you least expect it
that the sound of her name
instantly sounds like home
and that because of her
you learn to love again
this time, much better than before
fall madly in love and let it
unravel all of your expectations

A. N. Moore

You know the feeling you get
when thunder makes its debut

I was caught in a rainstorm
when she smiled up at me
as we met at the door

Lightning struck

And for the life I cannot remember
if it was the thunder or my heart
pounding in my eardrums

It was the way she smiled at me
my world turned upside down
my life, forever changed
she smiled
and my heart knew
nothing would ever be the same

A. N. Moore

I knew my heart was in trouble
but the kind of trouble
that makes your heart race

When you know this moment
is going to be something
that comes once in a lifetime

Even if you know it's risky
even if you know it's crazy

Your gut is telling you to fly

I seared into my memory
every inch of her face

Dare I say
my heart already knew
this was a moment of impact

-I'm ready to fly

I need to dream
only in colors of you
carry me away in the gentle moonlight
kiss me under cotton-candy skies

Love me here
love me there
and everywhere in between

I have dreamt the dreams
of many moons
of many suns

I have dreamt of picking
petals off flowers
only hoping to find the right one

The air was rich,
but how lucky am I
to have dreamt
of you;

My dreamcatcher
working overtime
to catch every
dose of you

-dreamcatcher

And I will remind myself
that only love is dangerous
if you make a monster out of it

Radical and mysterious things
deserve to roam free

-no containment

A. N. Moore

I told myself
not to fall so quickly

My heart knew better
from the last time
it dove in too deep

And sometimes that is the best thing
you can do for your heart

Look after it
and not utter those words too soon

So I waited
although I felt it
and a part of me knew
you felt it too

The good ones
are the loyal ones
with a wild side
and a heavy dose
of exactly what you need

I met you
and for the first time
in a long time
I did not want to question these feelings
instead I showered myself in them

-this love is safe

Back then,
we were nothing more than
a couple of kids
completely oblivious to the
impact of our very first kiss

And when we kissed
for the first time
I felt it everywhere

It was a spark
that turned
everything into
a raging fire

And I did not mind the flames

I laughed at the thought of
how many times I had undressed her with
my eyes and mind
before my fingers had a chance to follow

-confessions

A. N. Moore

Thoughts of you riddle my mind
flutters from my heart beat double time

My mind wandering

Wandering

Orgasm

-solo II

Day-dreamer
night-time thinker
it really does not matter
when every single thought is about you

You captivated my attention
not by a boastful ego
but the quiet serenity of your peaceful heart
and one of a kind soul

I craved all of your intimacy
every ounce of your spirit

I wanted to be consumed
in all that made up your love

-*everything*

It showed up
out of nowhere
for no reason
it is just there

It came
it left
it conquered

-anxiety

But to be expected
I began to assume that the phrase
some things are *too* good to be true

Would turn into a phrase I would use
when it came to me and you

When I would inevitably
spend days and weeks
getting over you

                    -pessimist

That emptiness
I so fondly remember
came rushing back to me today;
oh how time flies
but how little
does this feeling
fade away

It is so much easier now
to assume the worst
instead of expecting the best
love, up until this point, was salt
I had mistaken for sugar

-what do you expect?

Someone will eventually come along and show you
compassion, trust, and honesty
this is new, and sadly something society
is no longer use to

But you must
believe in them
trust in them
and let the love in

I promise you
that you will know who this person is
because you must remember
they are searching for you, too

So much of me is damaged
that parts of me
still recalibrate
to that old love
the not so safe love

It is not fair for you
to become a target
for the mistakes another
has made

I fear I no longer
know how to operate

You are not obligated
to untangle the misuse
of my emotions that have
nothing to do with you

But I am thankful
you are willing to stay

-safe

We could be rebels
you and I
even after our time
has faded to black and white
when the air is crisp
and the soul is full
when everything in this world
has dissipated into the abyss of nothingness
our love will still remain

This new love
it is scary

There is comfort in the past
That old love
has navigated its way
around my heart
so many times

To let a new love
forge new paths

It's scary
when it should not be
but it is

Because you do not know
how to navigate this new
found vulnerability

After an old love
had promised you
so many good things
and left you empty

-let this love in part II

This stubborn love
belongs with me
as much as it belongs to you
this stubborn love
is not made for anyone ordinary
and that is why it is ours

-extraordinary

I keep telling you
I love you
so that I can hear you say it back

To make up for all of the times
I was deprived of its true music

-reassurance

They tell you when you are younger
it is okay to be scared
of the monster under the bed
until one day they say *"no more nonsense"*

They warn you that now is when
the real monsters creep in;
anxiety, heartbreak, anger
and the fear to love again

The gang is all here
they are uninvited guests
that never needed a welcome mat

A. N. Moore

Why was I forcing
this new love to past
a test on an old loves
shortcomings

I am sorry
for ever forcing you
to believe you should
pay for someone else's mistakes

-self-sabotage

Our love is special
because we know
that love is not a game

A. N. Moore

The difference with you
was that you were patient
you were gentle
and you understood
where I was coming from

And in time
I learned some love is meant to teach you
and others are meant to hold you

You held my hand
instead of holding me back

And when I realized this
I finally let myself fall

-for you

Love Will Find You Elsewhere

No, it was not love at first sight
I do not believe in such things
I fell in love with you
the moment you said my name
and it felt like home

A. N. Moore

Your mouth dripped of a honey
I had never known

Those lips graced my skin
and I knew this love
was going to be different

-I'm on fire

Lay me on the table top
kiss me till my lips are numb
take me in mouthfuls
dripping off your tongue
fuck me like it's lust
even though we know it's love

A. N. Moore

Tangled tongues and limbs
the heat of the moment

Your tongue tracing over my most delicate skin

My heart pounds
my breath quickens

I am finally making love
this is not just sex

I understand now
why they say there is a *difference*

I asked what loving her
would feel like
she kissed me
dipped her finger on my tongue
and I tasted her wild

There was something about
me and you that clicked

In a way that others couldn't
I was not afraid to bare
my naked soul to you

To expose all of my truths to you

Just like me
you had every reason to doubt
every reason to question

But somewhere our hearts
had it out to prove
us both wrong

-I didn't mind letting them

Head case or not
the woman was desirable
simply undeniable
she was a little bit more than the usual
the type of woman I needed to have

A. N. Moore

I mean it when I say
I was never expecting to fall
not this soon

But as I kept
pressing the breaks
in fear of getting hurt
by calling it love before
it had time to bloom

The more my heart
surged up into my throat
twist my tongue to
form the words
letting them drip from my lips

I love you
I am ready to begin, again

If all I can write about is your heart
instead of your soul
my words do not reserve
the right to hold you

-soul food

A. N. Moore

Because me and you
we had this intimacy

One found through conversation
a real, honest, connection

Rarely ever seen
and even harder to forget

And that is the beauty of falling
in love with you

Wide-eyed adventurer
my wolf-skinned wanderer
found the wild in my soul
and called me home

Once I decided that falling for you was
inevitable
unstoppable

I thrived on the thrill of the chase
of wanting and craving
your one of a kind soul
to break apart this protective
shell I placed around my heart
so long ago

-freedom

This will hold me over, you will hold me through

elsewhere

I never had time for mediocre love
I wanted to drown in someone
I didn't just need her to look after my heart
I wanted her to envelop my soul

A. N. Moore

The soft dim glow of the early morning sun making its debut

Gave just enough light to expose your peaceful face

And as you slept I grazed your lips
with the gentle sweep of my fingertips
swiftly pulled you into my embrace
and I breathed you in
my world spinning madly

I am in love with you
truly
madly
deeply
before my day even begins

-good morning

In all my chaos
I found my peace
in loving you

-truth

I make no apologies
for falling in love with you
because it is

Real
authentic
and true

It did not matter how much time had passed
nor what people tried to say

This love was the real deal

I couldn't help it
she became a passion
a dream
a craving
she was love
and I was falling

A. N. Moore

Sadly, once you have made a mistake
of calling it love with someone
who was not the right one

Everyone will think
that you do not know any better

Thinking they are protecting you
they will blindly believe that
this new love is a mistake, too

So this love is forced to go to battle
even before it has the chance to thrive
like it wants to
like it needs to
like it should

We had a love affair with Sundays
where we would linger a little longer
kiss a little softer
and love one another a little slower

-Sundays

A. N. Moore

But what they don't know
is that this love
is something made of stardust
And everyone should be so lucky
to find a love like ours

-wish upon a star

And if I have grown to know anything
it is that my love for you will defy
all odds that say you and I
are not the real thing

A. N. Moore

Even if we try to tell them
it would not matter
because they will never understand what we
share when we are together

-and I am okay with that

Love Will Find You Elsewhere

Wrap your love around my heart
and let your body follow
let me swallow the sun
so I can be your center
let me swallow the moon
so I can shed light on all of your darkness

Because you have this gentle way
of letting me love you

Madly
Truly
Passionately

You had this gentle way of letting me
know it is okay to feel this...

-free

I wish I could go back and do it all over again
that first kiss
that first hello

I would relive every moment of it
just so I could watch us grow

A. N. Moore

I could wash the love we just made out of my hair

Scrub my skin
of your desire
and the wine-stained imprints
you left on my skin

I will soak my bones
but who am I kidding

Every part of you still lingers
my thoughts too dirty
to scrub clean

You've proven to be one hell of an addiction

She let me kiss soft promises on her heart
making me feel
for the first time
that I had finally found my home

A. N. Moore

What we shared between us
this mutual understanding
this freedom to let love
go where it needs to go

Needs no explanation
no validation

You did not control it
neither did I

We let it carry along
like soft jazz in the background
on a Sunday afternoon

There were no expectations
it was just me and you

-free part II

We should not go quietly
let this love be a catalyst
for earthquakes and thunder
let this love be a martyr
for the lost lovers and cynics
to believe in

-statement

A. N. Moore

Somethings have a way
of working themselves out
naturally

And with you
it was easy
it was simple
it wasn't forced

In every way
shape and form

Me and you
made sense

-easy

You are a gentle reminder that love has the power to heal
a heart that is this broken and worn
You are a gentle reminder that hopeless
romantics have every reason to remain hopeful

You came into my life
at the right time

Because even as a hopeless romantic
love was not my focus

I was not going to make you
into my whole world

We worked because
I knew whoever was going to love me
was going to know I was enough for myself

I no longer worried about
being enough for someone else

What you see is what you get
and you honored that

                    -a little perspective

I am sorry
I do not mean to dig, although I do
you are a mystery to me
and I want to know the ins and outs of you
your secrets, your scars, your light, your love

Love is deep rooted
it is not shallow
bring your shovel
I will bring mine too;
let's dig
let's uproot

Let's cultivate a love deeper
than just our bare skin

A. N. Moore

You were the first person
to tell me that there was a difference between
love being difficult
and love being hard

Tough times were going to come
rain was going to pour

But every day did not need to be a battle
not every day was going to be a struggle

Like it had been before

-I trust you

I am something like thunder
you are in awe of me
curious about something as magically terrifying
as the thunder in me

I cannot blame you
something powerful, authentic
a mystery
so raw, real, passionate

It is no secret
I am someone worth remembering

-thunder

It would not be fair
for us to find this love
this safe one

And not have to fight
not have to cry

Love is going to test you
whether the love is wrong or right

-adversity

I awoke in a dream
where we were on a road
that had light at the end
and an arrow saying
"this is how you please everybody"

I chased it for awhile
trying to reach the end
instead of reaching for your hand
as you reached for me
to admire the sunflowers
the birds and the bees

And before I knew it
I had lost you

I awoke the next day
with tears running down my face
I reached and pulled you into my embrace

-what are you reaching for?

A. N. Moore

Strike one:

you are women

(The lesser sex)

Strike two:

oh, lesbians

(Your duty is to procreate)

Strike three:

two different races should not mix

(because we still act like it's 1955)

How many more strikes
will everyone use as reasons to
dismiss this love, instead of honor it

-triple negative

Please tell me where I can find it
the big rule book of love;
show me where it says
every living
breathing, feeling being
should love based on gender
instead of soul

-I will never believe it

A. N. Moore

How many times
do we have to tell people
that the way we dress
has nothing to do
with our relationship

How many times
will I have to sit
here and say

Love is not gender
there are no roles
needing to be played

I am so sorry this is something
we still have to say

-gender roles

The best kind of love
is the one that comes unexpected
exceeds all expectations
and places an irreversible lock
on your heart

The important part is never apologizing for
loving someone that your heart has been
searching for

That is the thing about love
you can love her
you can love him

It is the visible act
the indescribable feelings
of hearts recognizing their counterpart

-there is no difference

There are more beautiful conversations to be had
within our silence;

I do not need the words
just let me feel
let me breathe in this love
let me taste your actions

-words do not do this love justice

A. N. Moore

The funny thing about all these battles is
they only seem to make our love stronger

-the joke is on all of you

My type of intimacy
is me and you baring our
naked souls not just our
naked skin

-drive me wild, love me crazy

A. N. Moore

Real love is not polite

The good ones
the real ones
the forever love

It's sacrifice
it's compromise

It is not supposed to be easy
it is not a walk in the park

Real love
it takes fucking work
it cannot be watered down
to teenage clichés

It isn't an ego boost
but a reality check

-real love, part I

You make me want to indulge
in the infinite and the forever

-glutton

Real love in the real world
is not polite
it's true

It will leave you naked
exposed and vulnerable
just to get the best out of you

Real love is finding comfort
in the uncomfortable conversations

It's letting go of hiding behind your doubts
and trusting the one you're with

Real love deserves better
than the moon and the stars

It's late night work
and early morning coffee

It's me and you
taking on the world together
our hands intertwined
our hearts on rhythm

-real love, part II

I've never really had a plan
and maybe that is what drove people crazy

I just wanted someone who wanted
to stick with me in my journey

Not hinder me
not stifle me

And trust that even if we are miles apart
it is not going to stop something
that is meant to be

-long distance

Maybe that is the advice we can give
when we are old and gray

That love shouldn't be looked for
maybe just hoped for

When the timing is right
and the heart is ready

You fight for that love
and you don't force your heart
to fit with someone who
was never meant
to play the part

-life lessons

It was real, wasn't it
this non-fairytale, fairytale

You and I
so real
so honest and true
we didn't need make-believe
nor did we need perfect
we just loved one another's perfect imperfections
honestly and wholeheartedly

And that is what separated us
from a love that just wanted the moon and the stars
instead of the roots and the soil;
a love planted, watered, cared for and bloomed
from the work of our own hands

-cultivate

A. N. Moore

It was everything it should have been
and then some

It was something like a dream
but not the cliché kind
where we rode off into the sunset

Fairytales never really interested me
because they never told my story;

The one of me and you
slow dancing in the kitchen
on a rainy afternoon
my hair a mess from the love we just made
and *Motown* playing in the background
as we laugh about my two left feet

The one with plenty of
imperfect, perfect, kisses
the ones that still send a spark up my spine
our lips navigating a love that still
sits needy on our tongues

The one of us sharing the real
the one of us
just as we are
just as we will always be

-in love

I craved your lips
and their conversation
as if kissing you
was its very own language
never lost in translation
when it came to me and you

A. N. Moore

I want to tangle
myself
up in you

But in the kind of way
that not only our legs
our lips
our tongues
and hands

But our hearts
would intertwine
and their rhythm would sync

I could love you
like this
indefinitely

Unravel me like your long lost favorite sweater
let me spill over you like your favorite cup of tea
open me like your favorite book
let your fingertips graze your favorite pages
read between my lines

-devour me

A. N. Moore

I will make love
to every inch of your mind

Your soul will follow as I pick up the broken
pieces others have tossed aside

I will strip away your insecurities
I will caress your weary heart
kiss away your scars
holding you together
while slowly letting you fall apart

Melt into my hands
let your levy finally break

-you deserve to spill

Let's go back
to the night where we were so alive
and so high on this feeling
where the stars aligned and it finally felt right

Let's go back
just to fall in love
with one another twice

I lose myself in
thoughts of you
in every song
and early morning cup of coffee
stirring around the idea
of how I got so lucky
to still be drawing hearts
around your name
when no one is looking

-forever

My greedy lips
kept begging for your kisses;
I was self-medicating
on the taste of your tongue

-addicted

A. N. Moore

Each love will teach you
something about yourself

What you truly want
what you truly need

You were the only one to ever show me
that the more I loved myself
the more you loved me

-with you I only keep blooming

Could I be naked with you
could I spill my soul
the way others will only
want to shed their clothes

Could we be naked
could we kiss away one another's scars
with poetic rhythm and depth

Could we be naked
expose our vulnerabilities
twist our desire
mold our lust
carve it into a love
that leaves us naked
even when we are clothed

-naked

A. N. Moore

This love
has taught me
that it no longer mattered about
my yesterdays but just today

Learning from one another
and loving you in different forms

That even when we disagree
we do so in a way that we are
respected and valued equally

We both had a seat at the table
to fight for the love that we share
to talk about the love that we need

-love languages

Love has to be like jazz
satisfying your soul;
highs and lows
sporadic
fast slow
let the melody take you
where it wants to go

-jazz

A. N. Moore

I've come to realize that so many people
think it's about these big things
you know, the big things

The big gestures
the grand romance

But you must remember it is the little things
that make up the big things

The way your hand
becomes second to their own
the one they always reach for
while they look at the stars
on long drives home

The way they make you dance
even if you have two left feet

The way they always call your heart home and how
when they tell you they love you

You can feel it ignite your soul

All I knew is that
I wanted to run with you
chasing after your hand
while we chased after our dreams

A. N. Moore

Everything about this love
whispers soft promises of forever

I did not need to worry about
being anything but being naked

In my mind
my body
my spirit

Where there once lived that feeling
that something would always go bad
like it had one too many times before   ·

I no longer needed to worry
because this time around
I had grown into my own
self-love and reassurance

I know that this where I am supposed to be

Love Will Find You Elsewhere

Imagine the first day of summer
when you wake up carefree, at ease
that freedom, that sigh of relief;
endless possibilities

-when you ask me what it feels like to love you

And it was not because I needed saving
as if you came in and swept me off my feet
rescuing me from my misery

I already saved myself
you just met me equally

Because that is what real love does
it makes room for you to grow

Side by side
never trying to steal
one another's sunshine

My dream is nothing more
than simply loving you
every morning, and each night
and as simple as it may seem
it will always be more than
enough for me

I finally felt safe
in this love that
we were in

So I carved out
a future with you
not in stone but in our soft embraces
and the tender caress of your heart

I carved out an everlasting love
with breathless kisses and tangled limbs

One where our love is not measured
by the amount of time we have spent together

But the memories collected under
the stars and the pale moonlight
and me and you dancing hand in hand
together, only us

-together

You taught me to fall to my knees in Faith
remembering there is a power much bigger
than what my own to hands were given to hold

-praying

A. N. Moore

It isn't perfect
this love

But it is ours
it keeps us coming back for more
because it is deep and it is strong

It has been a journey
you and me
we weathered one too many storms
we have seen the ugly

But our love has dug its
roots so deep
we have intertwined ourselves;
when you water yourself
you water me
it's a beautiful reciprocity

An imperfect love
finding beauty
in all its possibilities

-reciprocity

You call me your brown-eyed girl
they are endearing
dark and dangerous
but, oh, in the light
how they shimmer
oh, how they show the fire in me
they are something special
all because you see the magic in me

I will strive to always show you
that the love we share
is my greatest journey
my greatest accomplishment
and the most precious thing
I have ever had the pleasure
of calling my own

-6-24-17

My Beautiful Love
how infinite it all seems
when I walk with you hand in hand;
this love everlasting

We are never exactly right
where we think we expected ourselves to be

And we never really quite understand the journey
until we have gained some perspective on the past

So much of this journey
began in accepting
finding, losing, and rebuilding myself
into the person I am

So much of this journey
is moved through love

I have healed through writing
I've found comfort in a pen
and empty pages to make sense of what this life is

And when I began this journey
images of your face appeared
and when they ask me what my muse is
I will always tell them that it is you

-thank you

It was exquisitely simple
yet beyond powerful
and undeniably true:
every beat of my heart
was made for loving you

-simple

A. N. Moore

Maybe it is going to be found
in the last place you look

Sometimes we mistake it
take it for granted

Overlook it
deny it
hate it
defend it

We are all here searching for something
but it is time to
call off the search warrant

Because I promise
when you least expect it

-love will find you elsewhere

About the Artist

Justine Neves is a queer artist that predominantly works in illustration. The themes of her work address the joys and struggles regarding romance, desire, intimacy, relationships to others and self. Her work is conveyed through a queer lens that pulls from experience, where each drawing offers ambiguity for the viewer to relate and pour in their own perspective on its content. Justine has created art since she was a toddler, and has used it as an emotional outlet and a form of personal expression to this day.

She plans to continue to create art to connect with queer individuals and the world at large. Justine actively and passionately engages in local queer organizations, events and communities. She has a Bachelor's in Art and is currently completing her Masters of Science in Architecture. The architectural work she does strives to integrate sustainable and affordable life for as many as possible.

You can follow her creative work on Instagram: @justine_artworks

About the Author

A. N. Moore is an LGBTQ writer whose prose and poetry on social media have gained fans from around the world. Her relatable work has been praised for its sincerity on themes of self-love, LGBTQ, feminism, love, and more. She draws inspiration from her own experiences, the people she meets and the places she visits. She considers writing to be a therapeutic release of self-expression and self-love.

A. N. Moore is currently completing her Master's degree to become a Licensed Clinical Professional Counselor. She hopes, as she continues to embark on her own journey, that her work will inspire others in their own journey of self-discovery and healing. A. N. Moore is married to her high school sweetheart and strives to advocate for LGBTQ youth.

You can follow her creative work on Instagram: @anmooreword

Made in the USA
Lexington, KY
26 April 2018